# Ise Jingu

稲　塩　海　水　森　祈

# Ise Jingu

## and the **Origins of Japan**

text and photographs by
**Miori Inata**

SHOGAKUKAN

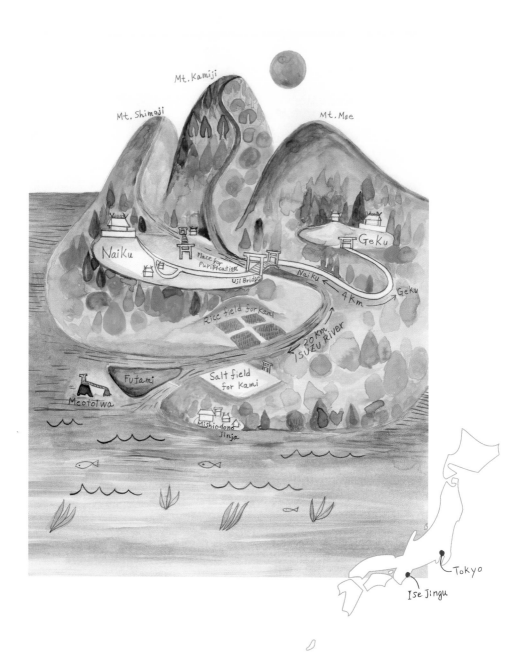

Published by Shogakukan Inc., 2-3-1 Hitotsubashi, Chiyoda-ku, Tokyo 101-8001

First edition, 2016

# Table of Contents

Part 1
# The Origins of Japan

CROSSING THE BRIDGE OVER THE ISUZU RIVER TO ISE JINGU
is like entering a time warp. It is, at once, a journey two
thousand years back to the origins of Japan, a moment to
appreciate the natural harmony in the present and a chance to
glimpse the potential of an attractive, sustainable future.

The sacred groves of Ise Jingu, surrounded by fertile
mountains and sea, have graced this location for centuries.
For more than 1300 years, this center of Shinto, Japan's
indigenous faith, has been maintained in its original form,
thanks to a unique ritual of renewal. The ritual, which
requires that the most important structures be rebuilt
every two decades, is an embodiment of the natural cycle of
life, of passing and rebirth. It also ensures that the ancient
philosophies and the skills required to follow the traditional
methods are carefully curated and passed down over
generations. Put simply, the structures standing here in the
forests of Ise are simultaneously very new—and very old.

Shinto reflects the deepest essence of the country. Blessed
with four distinct seasons, abundant water and a relatively
mild climate, some seventy percent of Japan is forestland. But
its precarious location on the Pacific Rim also means that the
country is often faced with frequent and sometimes hugely
destructive earthquakes, tsunami and other natural disasters.
As a result, Japanese have long been extremely sensitive to
nature; while in great awe of its power, they have learned to
accept both its abundance and its calamities.

The energy and life pulsing through nature are the
expressions of our deities, or what Shinto calls *kami*. Our beliefs
hold that the sun, the wind, thunder, the earth, mountains,
seas, trees and even stones—all the many manifestations of the
natural world, as well as some particularly impressive people—
are vessels of the kami. This is the root of Japan's reverence for
nature, a reverence with a long and deep influence on Japanese
thought, philosophy and aesthetic sense.

On the morning of the winter solstice, the sun rises in a
direct line over Ujibashi Bridge and the torii gate at the
entrance to Ise Jingu's Naiku sanctuary. Like all the other
structures, the wooden torii is replaced every twenty years,
with each pillar made from a massive *hinoki* tree trunk.

The official name Jingu is written with the characters for "kami" and "palace." While there are two large sanctums—the Geku and Naiku—that attract most visitors, these are actually just part of a larger landscape; the Ise area is also home to some 123 affiliated *jinja* (Shinto shrines) venerating a variety of important kami. In fact, Ise Jingu is actually an umbrella term for this complex, in which more than 1500 rituals are conducted every year. These rituals form the basis for Shinto. There are no revered founders, no dogma, no sacred texts—which separates it from other beliefs.

When I first visited Ise Jingu after many years spent overseas, I found something that forced me to rethink my approach to my life as a Japanese. I felt that somehow this was the origin of my own identity: that it was the basis of Japanese culture, philosophy, food, clothing and shelter—even today's technology.

It was not only the sight of what seemed to be the roots of the minimalist design and style for which Japan is famed. It was also the decorum and philosophy exemplified by the use of the word *do* ("way") that is used in the traditional cultures of the *sado* tea ceremony, *kado* flower arrangement and *budo*, the martial arts. I sensed all of these things—including the highly regarded Japanese cuisine—were deeply influenced by the sensitivities cultivated at Ise Jingu.

It also made me realize something else. Rather than thinking of humans as the "protectors" of nature, I began to understand that the nature that surrounds us is what gives *us* life. The Isuzu River, which passes through the environs of Ise Jingu, was a great help in this epiphany. Traveling along its twenty-kilometer length enabled me to grasp the cycle of life that it represents—as it has for more than two millennia—to pilgrims and other visitors to the area.

*Top:* From ancient times, the nearby sea of Toba has been famous for its pearls, its abalone and its seaweed, all used in offerings to the deities enshrined at Jingu.
*Bottom:* Even at times when crowds of pilgrims are visiting, this pond in the Naiku is a tranquil spot for relaxation and reflection, a place to experience the changing seasons.

The source of the Isuzu River, I found, is a nondescript small spring on the side of one of the holy mountains of the kami. The water takes life as it flows down through a forest of trees, both natural and cultivated, then through the sacred grounds of Ise Jingu. I followed it to where it enriches farmers' rice fields, then sprawls across a delta where workers harvest salt and eventually empties its mineral-rich waters into the sea itself. It is a thread that ties nature to humanity in a natural cycle.

The elements of the water's journey down the Isuzu form the basis of human life: the banks and vicinity provide the vegetation, the salt and the rice that is fundamental to our continuance. If "sustainability" is a keyword for us as we face a difficult future, it has long existed in Ise—and there is much to learn from its history.

The late evening summer sun reflects off the divine palace of the Naiku. Amaterasu-omikami, the deity of the symbol of the sun, has been enshrined at this peaceful location in central Japan for some two millennia.

# Part 2
## Water's Journey

# The **Source**

It is morning in Ise, and the eastern horizon over the sea
begins to brighten. Then the sun makes its appearance,
turning the mountains surrounding Ise Jingu a luminous pink,
even as the moon still hovers over the peaks. As the sun's rays
scatter their light through the virgin forest, the birds begin to
sing, and another new day begins.

As the day lengthens, the sun disappears behind a bank
of clouds. Then the heavens open, and rain begins to fall.
On the sacred peak of Mount Kamiji, each drop of water
makes its own small sound as it hits the surface, the first
step in its eventual voyage down the Isuzu River. Tree trunks
channel the waters from the sky down to the earth. The moss
underfoot turns a velvet green as it absorbs the liquid. Layers
of microorganisms and moldering leaves from the broadleaf
trees create a soft carpet that holds huge amounts of water.

Slowly the mountains' energy filters the water through the
layers of leaves and soil, until it eventually wells back up and
out of a spring. Then, little by little, the trickles of beautifully
pure water join to form a creek, which grows into a stream,
cascading through the rocks, chased by a cool breeze. The
watershed is home to a multitude of living creatures: fish, birds,
insects, deer, monkeys, boar.

Punctuated by waterfalls and twisting around boulders, the
water's flow gradually strengthens as it nourishes the forests
of the kami.

Much of Japan's plentiful precipitation comes during the
early summer rainy season, which ensures the mountains
surrounding Ise Jingu are a lush green for most of the year.
This drop is about to start its journey down the Isuzu River to
the sea. The mountains act as a huge natural filtration device.

The streams grow in size, tumbling over a number of falls,
the largest of them over ten meters in height.
*Right:* Because the virgin forest of the Ise Jingu area has been
protected so strictly over the years, botanists have found an
unusually large number of species of moss growing here.

# The **Natural Forest**

There are two kinds of woodland covering the mountains surrounding Ise Jingu. The virgin old-growth forest has been largely untouched for hundreds of years. It is surprisingly bright, with the leaves of the many trees reflecting the sun as they dance in the wind. This is the original form of Japan's forestland. Pristine natural forests are very rare today, and make up around one percent of the nation's woodlands. I traveled through the forest with permission and a guide from Jingu's forestry department.

Some sixty meters on each side of the river running through the mountains of Ise Jingu are deliberately preserved in their natural state to protect the purity of the water. There are evergreen broadleaf trees like camellias, camphor trees, *sakaki*, *shii* and *kashi* oaks—and conifers like *sugi* cedars and *momi* firs. There are also Japanese maples, chestnut and cherry trees.

There is a startling variety of vegetation in these mountains: 120 types of trees, 600 types of grass and 130 types of ferns. This is the only place that the native Chinese fringe flower is found in the wild in Japan.

The roots of the trees stretch far wider than the branches above, preventing the soil from eroding during heavy rains. It is a hallowed forest, perfect for prayer, a wellspring for the energy that created all life on our planet. It is a peaceful world, upon which the light of the sun descends.

*Right:* The octopus-like tangle of roots of a majestic hinoki tree rise off a rock with no obvious way to gain nourishment from the earth. The power of nature over the years has lifted this tree from its cradle in earth, but it has managed to stay beautiful and strong. This could well be the guardian of the mountain.

*Overleaf, left:* A hinoki shoot rises like a mountain fairy from a moss-covered stump: the beginning of a forest in miniature. Could this be the origin of the idea for bonsai? This birth of new growth on old is called "renewal," and it is critical to the life cycle of healthy forests. *Right:* The trees that surround Ise Jingu and many of Japan's jinja are all that's left of the country's virgin forest; rare treasures from ancient times.

# The Cultivated Forest

Ise Jingu's surroundings also include a cultivated forest, accessed by logging roads, that is off limits without special permission. This is where *hinoki* trees, used in the buildings' construction, are carefully tended, where nature is supported by human ingenuity. Eventually, all the lumber for the new structures will come from this area; presently trees from the Kiso region are also being cultivated and used in the building process.

Growing these trees requires a long-term perspective: five or more generations of caretakers are necessary to watch over each cycle of trees. Five years after planting, for example, the ground around the young saplings is cleared. Pruning starts after thirteen years. It is a process that far exceeds the capabilities of any one individual and the care of the trees is handed down over generations.

The forest's caretakers periodically perform the important task of thinning the growing trees to ensure that the largest of them grow quickly. They have learned that enhancing the young trees' access to natural sunlight is more important than fertilizer for the best growth.

The thinned forest is naturally seeded by bird droppings. The resultant growth of broadleaf saplings are allowed to grow as long as they don't interfere with the growth of the hinoki. This also helps maintain a natural hinoki/broadleaf balance, as the fallen leaves turn to humus and create rich soil.

The trees that are predicted to grow into the most useful lumber are marked by one or two painted white lines around their girth. Those expected to reach sixty centimeters in diameter over a lifetime of two hundred years get one line; those expected to reach one meter in the same timeframe get two. The painted rings act like the batons of a long-distance relay.

The cut trees are kept
submerged in water
for five years, causing
the wood to stabilize
and season as the water
content is reduced,
resulting in less deviations.
At a lumber workshop next
to the Geku sanctuary,
the master craftsmen
have carefully studied the
stored logs and marked
them for cutting. Each
piece is cut to perfectly fit
its destination as part of a
structure, and the skills of
the workmen ensure that
little of the wood goes to
waste after cutting.

# Rice-farming and Prayer

The raindrops that have fallen on Mount Kamiji have joined the stream of water emerging from the mountains, swelling the Isuzu River. Further downstream, it merges with Shimaji River, then flows through the grounds of Ise Jingu, where people scoop water from the banks for ablution rites. From there, it passes beneath the Ujibashi Bridge that delineates the border between where the kami dwell and where humans go about their daily lives.

Three kilometers past the Naiku sanctuary, the Isuzu reaches the town of Kusube, and a rice paddy that is affiliated with the Jingu. Since ancient times rice has been cultivated here for offerings to the kami. In an era long before food preservation techniques had been perfected, rice cultivation promised a regular food supply. The area's inhabitants shared the water according to annual conditions to ensure a healthy harvest. Competition would have meant too little for many; cooperation meant enough for all.

The crystal clear water of the Isuzu River makes its way through the grounds of the Naiku before continuing on its journey seaward. Worshipers use the waters for ablution rites, scooping handfuls from positions on the riverbank.

Just as Native
Americans believe
the gods have given
them corn, so
Japanese believe
rice is a gift from the
kami. In spring, the
blossoming of the
cherry trees signals
the time to prepare
for planting. The
fields are plowed.
Swallows swoop in to
peck at insects. The
seed rice is scattered
with prayers for a
bountiful harvest.
The seedlings
are ready by the
beginning of May,
when the people
of Kusube begin
planting the sacred
paddy. The blue sky
and white clouds
are reflected in
the water that has
been diverted from
the Isuzu to fill the
paddy. The quiet is
broken by the sounds
of ritual music; then
young rice-planters
bend to place each
and every seedling
carefully in the mud.

*Previous pages:* **Caressed by the wind, the rice-laden stalks sway in gentle waves. The waters of the paddy are a forest in miniature, home to pond snails, crabs, frogs and other living things. By the beginning of September, the once-green expanses of rice plants become flecked with gold. The harvest season has arrived and it's a time of joyous celebration. Rice is a gift from nature itself: the sun, the wind, the water and the earth.**

*Above:* **In the rice-gathering ritual, ears of the grain are reaped with great thanks for this year's safe harvest and prayers for the next. Summer clouds still tower above, but the darting and dancing of the red dragonflies signal the coming of fall.**
*Right:* **Bundles of harvested rice stalks, one twisted left, the other right, are tied with hemp thread and stored to offer to the kami.**

# Making **Salt** Downstream

The Isuzu River continues its journey downstream, carrying minerals from the sacred rice fields. Just before it reaches its final destination it passes through Shioai, where the river waters from the mountains meet the salt waters of the sea. Long ago, the ancients realized they could make finer, more mineral-rich salt by allowing seawater to intermingle with freshwater. Here at Shioai the salt fields run along the riverbank, and sacred salt is produced for the kami. Salt is critical to life—and in ablution rites and offerings at Ise Jingu.

Purified salt is created by utilizing the power of the sun and the moon; the ancient method is another example of man working hand-in-hand with nature. At high tide, water washes over the carefully prepared salt fields. At low tide, it leaves behind its treasure of salt on the sands, which is thoroughly mixed by hand.

This work happens just once a year, when the sun is at its strongest—and the surface of these salt beaches gleams like silver.

The final product of this ancient method of salt-making is called *katashio*—or hardened salt. The cakes are produced twice a year in spring and autumn for a total of two hundred. They are crushed when used as an offering in ritual ceremonies or for purification during formal worship. One cake, its surface dark from baking, fits perfectly in the palm of a hand.

Every day for ten days, local workers gather the salt-saturated sands *(left)* and pack them into the mouths of four buried jars covered in slatted sheets. Saltwater is then poured into the jars to concentrate it further. The salt is carried in barrels to the Mishio-dono Jinja, which sits in a pine forest overlooking the sea.

In the nearby salt-boiling area *(bottom left)*, workmen boil the water for several hours while making sure the salt doesn't stick to the bottom. The crude salt is then placed on an angled platform to remove *nigari* (magnesium chloride). It is then packed into bags woven of rice and barley straw, a combination that generations have learned is best for removing excess nigari and preserving the salt.

The crude salt, called *arashio*, is stored until it is time for the final stage in the salt-making process. A priest conducts a purification rite over the area, making an offering and reciting a Shinto liturgy in ancient Japanese. Then the salt is packed into pyramid-shaped earthenware vessels *(facing page)* for baking in a special furnace.

# The **Abundant Sea**

海

Finally, the water from the raindrops that fell on the Ise mountains reaches the sea, where the Isuzu River empties into the bay near Futami town and the *meoto-iwa*—the famed "husband and wife" boulders. The rocks serve as a natural torii gate as they guard over another sacred boulder beneath the waves. At the time of the summer solstice, one can glimpse an exquisite and mysterious landscape: framed by the rocks and silhouetted against the rising sun, the distant form of Mount Fuji can be seen.

A nearby jinja venerates the sacred boulder, and every year, when the sun is at its summer apex, holds a purification rite in the sea. Since ancient times, pilgrims have been purifying themselves on the beach of Futami before making their visit to Ise Jingu.

Thanks to the minerals carried down the river, the fertile ocean waters here are home to many species of shellfish. And just as in the hills at the river's source, here too are "forests": the kelp beds that provide a welcoming habitat for many creatures of the sea. It is another connection that exists between the mountains and the sea, forged over the length of the journey.

It is here that the power of the sun evaporates the seawater, creating towering white cumulonimbus clouds that fill the sky. As the clouds make their way towards the mountains, they darken once again, as the rumbling of thunder signals that a storm is coming. And as the first drops of rain fall on the thirsty mountains, the cycle has become complete.

The Isuzu River nourishes not just the forests. At Ise Jingu, it serves as a soothing, purifying form of prayer, a thread connecting the many things that give us life and are dedicated to the kami: rice, salt, vegetables and seafood. It is also part of a much larger cycle, for water, of course, covers seventy percent of the earth, and makes up sixty percent of our bodies. We represent but one part of this borderless system that nature has constructed for us.

The sacred "husband and wife" boulders near the spot where the Isuzu River meets the sea.

In the areas surrounding Ise Jingu, it is easy to absorb the naturalistic essence of Shinto philosophy, and the beauty and power of nature. Many years ago, a princess was sent by the emperor to find a suitable site where the most important deity, Amaterasu-omikami, could permanently dwell. After arriving in Ise, she received a revelation: "The land of Ise, of the divine wind, lapped by the waves from the eternal world, is a luscious land. In this land I wish to dwell." Little has changed: the waves still gently lap the shore and the seas off the nearby coast of Shima *(left)* supply many of the offerings used in rituals and ceremonies: abalone, oysters and seaweed.

# Jingu **Construction**

The architectural style of Ise Jingu has its origins in the raised grain storehouses of ancient times. And though there are similarities with Shinto buildings all over the country, the style reserved for the Jingu structures is called *yuitsu-shinmei-zukuri*, or "unique divine brightness style."

It is a style based on simplicity and straight lines, and, of course, natural materials. Some of the unique features are the *chigi*, the slender, gilded crossed rafters that jut out from the front of the roof, the *katsuogi*, the cylindrical billets riding across the ridge (originally meant to hold down the roof, though now decorative) and the *munamochi-bashira*, the massive columns supporting the ridge of the buildings.

It is difficult to grasp the scale of the wooden buildings from a distance, but the katsuogi, for example, are logs measuring 2.85 meters in length, with a diameter of 65 centimeters; the chigi extend almost 3.5 meters out of the roof surface.

The roofs are thatched with *kaya* grass, which takes five years of harvesting from the local forest to acquire the 25,000 bundles needed.

The simplicity of the buildings can be deceptive: the carpentry required in constructing them is incredibly difficult, using the most intricate system of joinery skills and working with extreme accuracy. Modern power tools are used for the less important work, but for internal surfaces that come in closer contact with sacred objects, all the work is done with traditional hand tools. The finished quality of the wood surface is absolutely exquisite.

*Fold-out:* The **Four Seasons** of Jingu

Part 3
# *Ise Jingu*

# Beyond the **Torii**

THE RIDGES OF MOUNT KAMIJI ARE ETCHED IN THE CRIMSON light of early morning as I pass through the torii gate and make my way across Ujibashi Bridge into Kotaijingu, also known as the Naiku. The tranquility of this place—the sound of waters rippling over the stone riverbed, the scent of the surrounding forest and the clean air—activates my senses. The rhythmic sound of my feet on the smooth gravel resonates deep within me, lulling my mind into a calm reverie.

After traversing the approach, I cross Hiyoke Bridge and enter the sanctuary itself. On the right is the font where one can cleanse mouth and hands in the ritualistic manner. Instead, I descend to the banks of the Isuzu and use its waters, filled with natural energy, for the ritual that qualifies me to approach something sacred.

Giant trees, centuries old, fill my vision as I make my way down the meandering wide pathway. Majestic *sugi* cryptomeria line the path, with virgin hinoki groves behind them; there are countless numbers within the hallowed area of Jingu, and the sheer scale of these magnificent living things dwarfs the humans walking among them.

I place my palm on one's trunk. The sense that this tree has been quietly watching over us for hundreds of years travels into my hand and on to my chest, filling me with comfort and awe.

Deep in the grounds lies the staircase leading to the main palace where the deity Amaterasu-omikami is venerated. From the top of the stairs I can see the simple lines of the wooden structure bathed in warm sunlight, its roof stretching beyond my vision on either side. I greet the kami in the traditional manner of prayer: two bows, two claps, a moment of silence with hands held together. As I pause, any thoughts of making a wish evaporate, and are replaced simply by a feeling of deep gratitude. Then I bow deeply once more.

The deep reverence for nature that marks the Shinto religion is clearly demonstrated by the way that these stately hinoki trees were not cut down to serve the needs of foot traffic, but left as a natural interruption of the wide gravel paths that wind through the complex.

What is this thankfulness that I feel here? I can only describe it as a sort of relief, a sense of returning to a place where one's soul can be at peace. Our planet is home to many inspiring and sacred sites, but I feel a special gratitude that such a place exists in the forests of Ise in my homeland.

The history of Ise Jingu extends back over two millennia. From the time of Japan's foundation by Emperor Jinmu, Amaterasu-omikami was worshiped as the deity of the ancestors of the imperial family and the symbol of the sun at the Imperial Palace in Nara. In the era of the tenth emperor, an epidemic swept through the land, and he decided to move the deity out of the Imperial Palace to a new location to worship more respectfully. Though the epidemic was then contained, it was only a temporary move, for the eleventh emperor sent one of his princesses, Yamato-hime, to search for a place where Amaterasu-omikami could be permanently and properly enshrined.

The princess traveled north, then south, inspecting some fifteen different locations. It must not have been an easy trip, but she was eventually guided to this fertile area of beauty and bounty from the land and sea. At a spot on the banks of the Isuzu River, she received a revelation: "The land of Ise, lapped by the waves from the eternal world, is a luscious land. In this land I wish to dwell." The spot became the location of the current Naiku of Ise Jingu—the eternal resting spot for Amaterasu-omikami.

A few kilometers away is the Toyo'uke-daijingu, also called the Geku, which venerates another deity, the guardian of clothing, food and housing. The kami, Toyo'uke-no-omikami, came to the area some 1500 years ago to serve food to Amaterasu-omikami. These two sanctums are what most people envision when they think of Ise Jingu.

*Facing page:* **The ablution ritual: hold the ladle with the right hand to pour water over the left; switch hands and do the same to the right hand; switch hands again, pour in the left hand and take a small sip before spitting it out.**

*Overleaf:* **The main palace of the Naiku, venerating Amaterasu-omikami. This was taken before the deity's transfer from the former site, which is why I was allowed to shoot from so close. There are five layers of the wooden fence seen surrounding this sacred area.**

JINGU IS A SITE WHERE RITUAL PLAYS A HUGE ROLE: IN FACT, rituals and ceremonies are conducted more than 1,500 times a year. Many are related to the annual rice crop, with prayers for sowing, growing and harvesting. The most important of them, called Kan'namesai, dedicates the recent harvest to the kami as a message of gratitude, and lasts for eleven days from October 15 of each year. Rice that the Emperor himself has tended is brought to Jingu, new costumes are made for the priests and new tools are crafted for the ceremony. Much of the ritual takes place in darkness lit only by flickering torches, as priests prepare a ritual meal for the kami, a scene made even more mysterious by the complete silence that surrounds it.

But the most spectacular ceremony of all spans the entire area of Ise Jingu, lasts for ten years and encompasses the work of thousands. It is an ancient ritual of renewal and rebuilding called Shikinen Sengu.

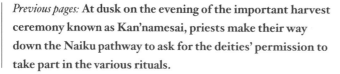

*Previous pages:* **At dusk on the evening of the important harvest ceremony known as Kan'namesai, priests make their way down the Naiku pathway to ask for the deities' permission to take part in the various rituals.**

One of the important ceremonies of Kan'namesai begins
around ten p.m. at the Naiku. The flickering torchlight
illuminates the priests' robes while they go through the steps
of the ceremony. It is a hauntingly beautiful ritual, in which
prayers of gratitude are offered to Amaterasu-omikami,
along with sacred rice harvested from the crop tended by
the Emperor himself. Rice, sake and locally gathered foods,
such as abalone, lobster and vegetables are included in
the offerings, symbolizing the self-sufficient nature of the
rituals. All the priests' robes and tools are newly made for the
year's paramount ceremony.

# The Cyclic Rituals of the Shikinen Sengu

The American architect Antonin Raymond, a student of Frank Lloyd Wright, once said, "The world's oldest and newest buildings can be found deep in the forests of Ise."

He was speaking of Jingu and the unique ritual—the Shikinen Sengu—for which it is renowned. Every two decades, the two main sanctums, along with fourteen superior affiliated jinja, are completely rebuilt as exact jinja following ancient architectural styles and methods. This is followed by the reconstruction of 109 affiliated jinja, and after the construction is complete, each of the deities is moved to their new location. Over thirty rituals are performed before the main ceremony to transfer the deities to their new abodes.

This entire process takes an incredible ten years to complete; and the complex construction techniques include, for example, embedding logs in their natural state into the ground as stilts. It is an architectural style that follows the traditional raised-floor design that was used for grain storage buildings. The twenty-year cycle keeps the structures in peak condition while ensuring they remain in their original configuration in perpetuity. This unique ritual combines sustainability and renewability—for after the buildings are disassembled, the lumber is sent to other jinja around Japan for use in their own buildings. The thickest pillars from both sides of the main buildings in the Naiku and Geku will be used to build the torii gate at the entrance that will remain for the next two decades.

Next to each structure in Ise Jingu are identical plots of land where the next incarnation of the building will be constructed. In the middle of each lot is a small structure marking the center of the future main building.

The Shikinen Sengu is a magnificent ritual that has continued for over 1300 years. It began in 690 AD, the era of

This small structure, called the *shin no mihashira no ooiya*, stands in the center of the plot where the new main building will be constructed, and protects the location of the central pillar.

the forty-first Emperor, but the precise reasons why remain a mystery. One theory is that it matches the twenty-year period of the shelf life of stored rice. Another is that it is based on the durability of man-made structures of the time. Others believe that twenty years marks the turning points of life, and also marks the ideal time period for passing along knowledge and skills to new generations. There are many theories, and they all make sense. So perhaps Emperor Tenmu and Emperor Jito simply intuited the laws of nature and established the system to ensure a perpetual cycle for future generations to follow. I personally feel that it represents their guidance for us to live within the natural cycle of life.

Regardless of the original reasons, the result is that the skills needed for the rituals and offerings have been passed down over many generations. The *miyadaiku* carpenters, for example, begin apprenticeships in their twenties, are officially recognized in their forties and then become masters in their sixties. This is also true of the craftsmen and artistans who make the many items used as offerings: swords, lacquerware, textiles and other traditional crafts. The twenty-year cycle acts as an excellent time frame for each generation to perfect all of the critical skills and knowledge required.

In other words, while the structures and the offerings are new, knowledge, skills and history accumulated from some thirteen centuries are part of each and every item.

The following pages cover the major events, which I photographed over a ten-year period beginning in 2005.

The Shikinen Sengu ritual calls for reconstructing and recreating buildings, tools and the large number of offerings that are made using ancient traditional craft skills. This requires the master artisans to pass on their talents and knowledge to each new generation, a practice that has been followed for centuries. In this way, the ritual is responsible for maintaining the high quality craftsmanship of such traditional arts as weaving silk obi for swords, a process that takes one year of painstaking work for each obi *(top)* as well as the complex, detailed woodwork that goes into the buildings' joinery *(bottom)*.

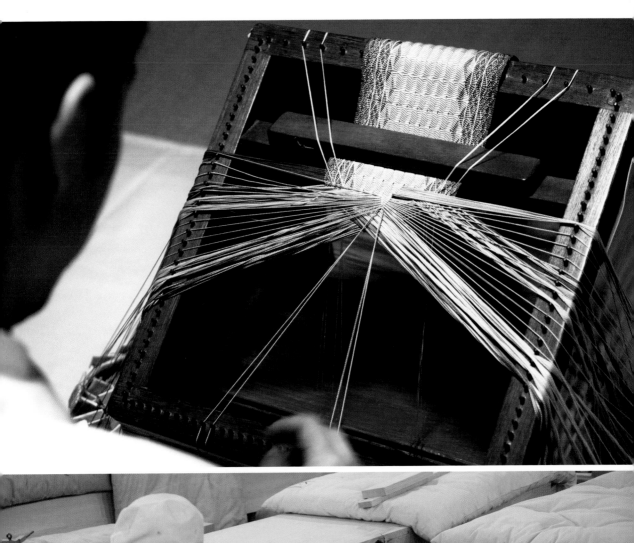

Years One and Two
## Harvesting and Carrying the Logs

The Shikinen Sengu begins on the second day of May with the Yamaguchi-sai ritual that pays respect to the mountain deity residing in a boulder at the foot of Mount Kamiji.

That night, another ritual is held to pay respect to the deities of the trees as they are felled for use as the sacred core pillars in the center of the new sanctuary structures. This ritual is carried out in secrecy in the dead of night in the forest of Ise Jingu. On September 19, a ceremony is held in the Geku for the cut trees that are used to make an outer container for the box holding the holy mirror. The wood is also carried to Jingu. The ritual's site is exquisite in its simplicity; a mat on the ground and nothing else *(above)*. The sunlight, filtered by the branches above, shimmers where it illuminates the ground. The breeze is fresh and clean, and the rustle of foliage and the birdsong mingle to create a wonderful background of sound. I have never felt so alive, nor have I ever seen anything that has stoked such a sense of mystery.

Most regular rituals are performed first in the Geku, then the Naiku. But for the Shikinen Sengu, it is the other way around.

*Facing page:* Other trees to be used in the reconstruction process are felled after many rituals in the Kiso Valley National Forest. The woodcutters use an ancient technique called *mitsuo-giri*: three woodcutters simultaneously cut into the sides of the trunk, leaving only three sections emanating from the core. Then one of the remaining sections is cut, causing the tree to topple, and filling the air with the rich aroma of hinoki wood.

After felling the tree in the Kiso forest, branches from the top of the tree are stuck in the center of the severed trunk as a show of respect for the cycle of the tree's life. It is more a token of gratitude than an official ritual, but I was moved by the sensitivity behind the act. Moments after this photograph was taken, the skies opened and a thunderous rainstorm soaked everyone at the site. I felt the kami were reacting to what had just taken place there. Then the wood for the box is transferred from Kiso to Ise.

The second year of the preparations features a ceremony in which people drag the consecrated logs into the Naiku and Geku. A storm had swept through the area the day before, swelling the Isuzu River, so that participants had to pull the logs for the Naiku sanctuary through waist-deep waters (facing page). Dozens of participants, young and old, male and female, cooperated in hauling the logs, accompanied by the beautiful rhythm of the *kiyari* lumberjacks' chants. That it takes places during the cherry blossom season makes the scene all the more impressive.

The logs intended for the Geku sanctuary must travel over land, and the sacred forest is filled with the sound of the carts' creaking wheels echoing through the trees on their way to start their "new lives" as parts of the buildings.

At the end of April, another ritual marking the beginning of construction is held to pray for safety during the long building process. And in September, a ritual is held in the Kiso mountains asking the kami of a tree for permission to cut it in order to make another container for the holy mirror. This one is used during the transfer between the old and new divine palace.

## *Praying for the New Plots*

The *chinchi-sai*, or "ground-consecrating ceremony," offers prayers to the kami of the plot of land where the new building will be constructed and includes prayers for the safety of the workers. This is the first time that photographers were allowed to shoot pictures of the site, and I was stunned at the size of the temporary building that had been erected to cover the central pillar. The center and four main points of the compass are marked with strips of cloth: red (southeast), yellow (center), white (southwest), purple (northwest) and green (northeast). Along with the traditional folded white paper streamers called *shide*, they flutter softly in the breeze. The participation of young boys and girls *(below),* called *monoimi*, add freshness and purity to the proceedings.

## Year Five
### *Rebuilding the Bridge*

The fifth year is when the Ujibashi Bridge leading to the
Naiku is rebuilt. The massive timbers used to construct the
bridge, which handles millions of pilgrims over its lifetime,
were still in fine shape, but this too is part of the renewal
process. When complete, the surface is as smooth and shiny
as silk, and the aroma of the fresh hinoki used for its trusses,
girders and deck fills the air. The new bridge is consecrated
by the feet of three generations of one family and their wives,
who are the first to walk over it in a crossing ceremony.
This symbolism of the ritual clearly expresses the concept
of Shikinen Sengu—the importance of handing over the
knowledge and skills required from one generation to the
next. Being one of the first to cross this new bridge after the
ceremony was quite an experience, one that I will not forget.

## Year Eight
### *Building the New Sanctums*

The year is marked in March by the sound of the wooden mallets of the *miyadaiku*, the "Shinto shrine carpenters." These workmen are experts in the art of Shinto shrine carpentry, which requires extensive knowledge and well-honed skills, including difficult joinery techniques. The first ceremony to mark the start of building celebrates the erection of the pillars, and the sound of the mallets echoes through the forest. That same day, priests conduct a second ritual to attach the *gogyo*, a sheet of metal that has been polished to a mirror-like shine, under the gables at both ends of the main palace roof.

Priests and carpenters gather twenty-two days later in both the Naiku and Geku sanctums. The framework of the main palace has already been raised so they reenact the motions of building. Various steps are recalled, from finding the precise locations for the ridgepoles, to raising them—represented by pulling two long, white cloths *(right)*.

The priests stand in the west, the carpenters in the east, and they pull white cloths as if raising the ridgepole while other carpenters gather on the roof, tossing rice cakes and bellowing, "A building for a thousand years! Ten thousand years! A million years and forever!"

Two months later, construction has reached the point for holding a ceremony to begin work on the thatched roofs: two months after that the buildings are fitted with metal ornaments in another ceremony.

Year Nine
## The Final Preparations

A number of preparatory rituals are held in the two months leading up to the *sengyo*, the core ceremony in which the deities will be transferred to the newly constructed palaces after eight years of labor—among them the Shogu *(facing page)*, which is the main sanctuary of the Geku. There are ceremonies to bring new white pebbles for the grounds and to make the hole for the key of the sacred door of the new main palace. There is a ceremony in which priests carry the receptacle housing the container that hosts the holy mirror—the symbol of the kami—into the main sanctuary. There are rituals purifying the buildings, to place the sacred core pillar at the center of the main sanctuary, and one that ensures a solid fit for the base of the new building's pillars.

Then, on October 1, a ceremony is held to celebrate the end of construction. In the afternoon, the priests change their attire from simple white to brightly colored robes. One rite is held to confirm that the divine treasures created by the craftsmen and artisans as offerings are in accordance with tradition. The priests themselves, along with the new items of offerings, take part in a purification ritual in the forest next to the Isuzu River. On this occasion, the rain came down quite heavily, drenching the gathering in what seemed to be nature's assistance in the purification. Then the new palace is decorated with the offerings, sacred apparel, furnishings and divine treasures in preparation for the transfer ceremony.

Only after all these rituals are completed can the core ceremony take place, the transfer of the deities to their new homes.

*Following pages:* The Mito-sai ritual, which celebrates the completion of the door, consists of priests offering a meal to the kami. The menu includes the blessings of nature found in the land of Ise: rice, sake, salt, vegetables, lobster, fish and seaweed.

*Facing page, top:* The day before the sengyo ceremony, priests change their costumes from plain white to striking colors, and parade to the main sanctuary of the Naiku for one of the last rituals—confirming that the new divine treasures that will be offered to the kami are in accordance with tradition. *Bottom:* A ceremony for purifying the new divine treasure is held at the Naiku the same afternoon on the banks of the Isuzu River, performed by priests using evergreen branches. The sister of the Emperor attended the ceremony.

*Above:* Another ceremony for purifying the new divine treasure is held three days later in the Geku. The Emperor's daughter attended this ceremony.

# The Sengyo Ceremony

THE *SENGYO* CEREMONY OF THE MOST RECENT SEKINEN SENGU
was held in the Naiku at eight p.m. on October 2, 2013, some
eight years after I began photographing Ise Jingu. That night,
when the lanterns were extinguished, plunging the entire
area into pure darkness, I felt as if I was standing in the
center of the universe. Re-enacting the *Amano-iwato biraki*,
a mythological story in which the "cave of the heavens" was
opened, a priest crowed like a rooster three times and his
cry echoed through the sacred forest. Amaterasu-omikami
had departed the present residing palace. The stars overhead
shimmered brighter than ever. The life in the forest around
us stirred. The host of the kami, covered with white silk, was
carried to the new palace to the accompaniment of beautiful
traditional Shinto music.

   I was greatly moved by the realization that what was
transpiring before my eyes were precisely the same ceremonies
that were performed 1,300 years ago, every twenty years since,
and will continue to unfold again and again in the future.
Right then, as Amaterasu-omikami took up residence in the
new palace, a grateful wind swept through the area.

   The transfer of the deities at the main sanctuaries ended
that October, while the transfer at the affiliated jinja was to
continue through March of 2015. While these ceremonies
marked the "end" of the Shikinen Sengu, they also marked the
beginning of the new twenty-year cycle into a beautiful future.

The great ceremony, Sengyo, of the long process of renewal
known as the Shikinen Sengu. This is the moment at the
Geku when the kami was moved from the previous site to
the new palace It is performed in the dark of night, with the
ceremony illuminated only by torchlight. It was the climax of
my decade-long, photographic journey following the process.
The mysterious ritual under the stars and the towering
canopy of trees was deeply moving.

# Afterword

IN 1991, I MOVED FROM MY HOME IN JAPAN TO NEW YORK
City, where I spent the next ten years. The city is unique—a
metropolis where one can experience any number of different
cultures simply by walking to the next block. Taking a stroll
there is like traversing a miniature globe—from the famed
Little Italy and Chinatown, to Koreatown and other enclaves
where Russians, Indians, Poles and other nationalities
congregate. I began to feel that if only the rest of the world
could adopt this lifestyle and mind-set, free of discrimination,
where mutual understanding arises from casual friendships,
that there would definitely be less conflict and suffering. I
truly believed it was an experiment in co-existence that had
been bestowed upon humanity.

But that belief evaporated in massive clouds of smoke as
I watched the terrorist attack of 9/11 from my apartment
window. I spent the following year in a haze of depression,
before eventually coming to the realization that there must
be a key to peace somewhere out there. On a trip to a Native
American sacred site, I felt my soul salved by the natural
surroundings, and I found myself instinctively reaching for
my camera—which had lain untouched for more than a year.

I began a pilgrimage in search of answers—to Jewish, Islamic,
Christian, Orthodox Christian, Buddhist and Hindu holy
sites around America, the Middle East, Europe and Asia. I
prayed along with the believers and photographed what I saw.

At a gallery exhibition featuring my photographs in Tokyo's
Ginza in the summer of 2005, I met a university professor
who was knowledgeable about Shinto. He suggested that I
photograph the Shikinen Sengu series of rituals that were
beginning that year. The next week, I was introduced to
someone in the international division of the Jinja Honcho
Association of Shinto, and I visited Ise Jingu for the first time
in my life in late August with them.

I knew almost nothing of Ise Jingu, but the moment I set
foot on its grounds I could tell that it was an exceptional
place. The various jinja on the premises were named for

The main palace of the Geku.

natural phenomena, including the jinja of winds (*kaze-no-miya*), the jinja of earth (*tsuchi-no-miya*) and the deity of waterfalls (*takimatsuri-no-kami*). I soon knew that I had made an important connection.

As the gravel on the path to the Naiku crunched beneath my feet, I felt enveloped by something soft and warm. When I stepped into the sanctum, I felt my senses enhanced; it was as if I was aware of every particle in the air—and tears filled my eyes. Something bigger than myself was watching over me and welcoming me back. I realized that a key to harmony existed in my homeland of Japan, and I felt driven to learn more about Ise Jingu and to photograph it.

During my time living abroad, I had often felt a lack of knowledge about my own country. I knew that I needed to learn more about my roots in order to know who I was, and to become a more international person. My visits to Ise Jingu quenched that thirst and filled me with happiness. Jingu's simplicity is strong and beautiful, and it speaks to me deeply with its energy. It is very much alive, and its visage changes with the seasons.

I returned numerous times after my first visit, losing myself in my photography. Even after all these years, I suspect I have only scratched the surface of potential learning. I did learn to appreciate every moment of my time spent in this "real" Japan, with its unique approach to eternity.

I WORKED ON THE PROJECT FOR TEN YEARS, FOLLOWING THE many rituals of the renewal. During the process, for a brief time in 2013, the new and old buildings stood side-by-side. Plants were sprouting from the roofs of the old buildings, as if they were already beginning to return to the forest. The new jinja glowed with the sheen of the recently cut wood. The old and new, worn and bright, side by side, beautifully portrayed the essence of the twenty-year natural cycle.

I finally finished shooting the Shikinen Sengu on March 16, 2015, with the renewal of the affiliated jinja.

I had photographed as much as I was permitted, and had learned a great deal from the experience. I learned of the importance of maintaining balance. But more than anything, I was constantly reminded of the significance of "cycles."

The main palace of the Naiku.

All of nature—from the quantum level to the entire universe, is cyclical. It is through cycles that everything is organized and harmonized.

As I followed the reconstruction ritual, Ise Jingu revealed its own grand cycle, one based on passing everything on to the next generation, and connected to the Shinto concept of *tokowaka*, or "eternal youth," representing true eternity. It is a symbol of the cycle of reproduction, something that, to me, seems the essence of life itself.

Shinto belief holds that everything is host to a deity, and people pray to what are referred to as "the eight million deities." The beliefs are not about protecting nature from a dominant position; instead they are about instilling us with the knowledge that we are simply a part of the world around us.

Nature is at its most awesome and most beautiful when it is in its natural state. When we are attracted to certain trees, it is because we are appreciating the way they exhibit a delicate balance by stretching their branches to maximize the amount of sunlight received by their leaves. When we admire the beauty of snowflakes, it is because there is a harmony between the unique shape of every one and the perfect process of their development.

I feel that Ise Jingu is the ultimate expression of humans not only living in harmony with nature, but living "as" nature. It is an expression of something more than a religion. It is a philosophy based on the Earth's place in the universe, and our place on Earth. It is a sense of something beyond reason and understanding, guiding us how to live as citizens of this planet. It has much to teach us about symbiosis, harmony and regeneration.

Like anyone else who follows the news, I have been watching as our world is increasingly wracked by horrific events. I have the feeling, however, that Ise Jingu and the philosophy it represents could serve as a beacon of light for humanity, becoming not only a treasure for Japan, but for the entire world.

# Author **biography**

MIORI INATA graduated from Tama Art University in Tokyo, having majored in oil painting. She taught fine arts for a number of years in Tokyo before relocating to New York in 1991. After a photography course at Southampton University, she began her career with a camera, focusing on the people of New York and the city's culture. Her life changed after watching the tragic events of September 11, 2001 from her apartment window, and she began what was both a personal and professional pilgrimage—travelling the world to photograph sacred religious locations in order to understand the relationship between humans and deities and find the key to peace. This eventually led her to the most revered site of Japan's Shinto religion, Ise Jingu, where she spent over a decade capturing its essence through its rituals and ceremonies.

This is Inata's sixth book (her first in English). Her photographs have appeared in a number of periodicals, including the *Washington Post*, *Vogue Japan* and *Aera*. She has held exhibitions at the United Nations, Columbia University, Brooklyn Botanical Garden, Harvard University, Tokyo National Museum, Shanghai Asian Society, the Israel Museum and many other locations.

*Visit her website at www.mioriinata.net*

# Acknowledgements

I would like to say thank you to Ise Jingu, and all of the people there who accepted me and shared so much of their knowledge. A special thanks goes to the Shinto Priest Shinnyo Kawai, formerly the head of the public relations division. Also to forest manager Katsuhiko Kurata, who guided me through the mountains.

My deepest gratitude goes to Tokyo Daijingu (*www.tokyodaijingu.or.jp*), particularly Chief Priest Fumihiko Matsuyama, for the unending support of this project. This book would not exist without their help. Thanks also to Takayuki Ashizu, now Chief Priest of Munakata-Taisha, and Nozomi Terao, Prof. Yasuhito Hanadoh and Masayoshi Miyanaga. They enabled my first visit to Jingu. I always appreciate the continued support and assistance from Motomi Nakamura, Tazuko Kiba, Akiko Hanada and Keisuke Kikuchi, and I am very happy to have been able to work with my editor, Gregory Starr, designer Andrew Pothecary and editor Naoyuki Wasaka of Shogakukan.

---

Ise Jingu and the Origins of Japan

2016年5月1日　初版第1刷
著者　　稲田美織
発行人　菅原朝也
発行所　株式会社小学館　〒101-8001 東京都千代田区一ツ橋2－3－1
TEL 03-3230-5438(編集)
　　　 03-5281-3555(販売)
印刷所　凸版印刷株式会社
製本所　株式会社若林製本工場

© Miori Inata, 2016. Printed in Japan
ISBN978-4-09-103237-9